# My Soul Speaks

## Unsaid I am

Dr.Adyata Dave Trivedi

BookLeaf Publishing

India | USA | UK

Made with ❤ on the BookLeaf Publishing Platform
www.bookleafpub.in
www.bookleafpub.com

# Dedication

Dedicated to,

For the voices lost in silence, and the hearts that whisper truths no one hears.

To every soul that speaks without words, and lives without needing to be seen.

To the inner light that never dims, even when the world looks away.

For the quiet strength within me, and all who carry their stories in silence.

To those who feel deeply, speak softly, and still burn bright from within.

# Preface

*In the quiet places where words falter and silence lingers, the soul begins to speak. "**My Soul Speaks - Unsaid I Am** "is a journey into the unvoiced depths of self—those truths that live beneath the surface, waiting for the stillness to rise. This poem is not just a telling, but a becoming. It is a reflection of identity, memory, emotion, and essence—woven together in the language of feeling. Each line reaches inward, each verse listens to what cannot always be spoken aloud. It is a voice from within, finally finding breath.*

# Acknowledgements

I am grateful to the moments of stillness that gave my soul space to speak.

To the people—seen or unseen—who inspired courage in silence, thank you.

To the pain that taught me depth, and the healing that gave me voice, this poem is born of you.

And to the inner self I once ignored—thank you for waiting.

All poem based of life events which directly or indirectly related to everyone.

I am thankful to My parents,My sister,My in laws and My husband , My Darling Daughter and Everyone who connected to me directly or indirectly.

# 1. Unsaid I Am

I do not speak in thunder—
But in the hush, where silence lingers under.
Where stillness holds its breath,
I become, unspoken, beneath the depth.
I am not the echo of what's expected,
Nor the shadow of dreams redirected.
I rise from roots that none can see,
Growing wild, alone, and free.
My voice is not always sound—
Sometimes it's silence that is found.
Sometimes it trembles, quiet and deep,
In a hand that doesn't reach or keep.
I carry memories stitched in thread,
Woven in feelings I've left unsaid.
Words left behind, whispers in the dark,
Folding like secrets, leaving a mark.
You may not hear me, but I stand tall,
Speaking in glances, I won't fall.
In the spaces between, in the way I stay,
Refusing to vanish, I make my way.

I am not silence, though it may seem,
I am the meaning of every dream.
Not lost, but layered in layers of time,
I rise, steady and prime.
I speak not to be heard or seen,
But to be known in ways serene.
My soul speaks unsaid—
And still, I am, not dead.
From within, I rise again.

# 2. Wordless world within me for You

**for my parents,**
**I am shaped by your quiet sacrifices,**
By the strength you wore, pure and priceless.
By love you gave, without asking a thing,
Love that soared, on invisible wings.
**You are my parents, my guide, my friend,**
My shelter, my life, on you I depend.
You taught me to listen, to hear the call,
To stand in the silence, not fear it at all.
**To carry my dignity, quiet but strong,**
To stay grounded, though the world moves along.
When my voice was lost, and words felt too few,
You gave me space, and helped me break through.
**When I hid behind smiles, kept feelings inside,**
You saw through it all, never let me hide.
Now I speak with the heart that you made,
With courage and love, in the light you laid.
**Every dream I carry, unsaid but true,**
Bears your fingerprints, they're part of you.

You are the root where my strength is sown,
The reason my soul dares to stand, full-grown.
**So if I seem silent, with words left unsaid,**
Know it's from you, in your care I've been fed.
From patience, from love, from all you've bestowed,
I speak from the strength that you've helped me unfold.

# 3. Beneath the surface My In-law Parents - but Parents

In your quiet acceptance,
I found a home, soft and constant.
Not built with walls, but hearts that shine,
With warmth, with grace, with love divine.
You never asked me to become more,
Just to be myself, nothing more.
Yet through your kindness, kind and true,
I became more, thanks to you.
Your presence has been steady, always near,
A comfort found, with nothing to fear.
A gentle strength that asks no praise,
Yet gives so much, in countless ways.
Through unspoken blessings, shared with care,
Through quiet meals and moments rare,
I learned that family, near or far,
Is made of love, not blood, by star.
My soul has grown in your steady light,
Softly, gently, through day and night.
Learning the language of care so pure,

In every moment, love's allure.
If I speak with calm, if I move with grace,
It's because of you, in this sacred space.
You've shown me love, not loud but true,
In silence, love speaks anew.
I am from within, yet now I know,
A piece of you in me will grow.
In quiet love, a seed is sown,
Forever, I carry what you've shown.

# 4. My voiceless piece of heart  for my sister

There are pieces of me
that only you have ever truly seen—
the cracks, the chaos,
the quiet dreams I never dared to name.

You've been the keeper of my unspoken truths,
the one who stood beside me
when I didn't know how to stand for myself.
You never asked me to explain—
you simply stayed.

In your laughter,
I found my light again.
In your silence,
I found a shelter stronger than words.

You've carried parts of my pain
without ever letting me feel the weight.
You've celebrated my joy

like it was your own heartbeat.

We are different in ways the world may notice,
but in ways that matter,
we are made of the same soul-stuff—
stitched together by memory,
bound by something deeper than time.

You've shaped my voice
just by being who you are—
soft, fierce,
and endlessly giving.

And if I speak from within now,
with truth, with grace,
with love that doesn't always need to be loud—
it's because I learned it watching you.

My soul speaks unsaid—
and in the quietest places of who I am,
you are there.

# 5. I kept within that you are my Sister in law but my sister

They say we don't choose our in-laws,
but if I had the chance—
I'd choose you every time.
Not just for the laughter
or the easy conversations,
but for the way you make family feel
a little more like friendship.

You understood me
before I had to explain myself—
which is both comforting
and just a little suspicious!

You've been a quiet cheerleader,
a secret-keeper,
and the perfect partner
for sharing knowing glances at family dinners.

You remind me that love
doesn't always come with big words—
sometimes it's in the shared snacks,
the inside jokes,
or the random messages just to say,
"I saw this and thought of you."

My soul may be soft-spoken,
but it's laughing louder
because you're in my life.
And somewhere in the heart of who I am,
you've taken up your own little corner—
full of warmth, wit, and way too much chai.

So if my soul speaks unsaid,
know that you are part of that quiet joy
that lives deep within.

# 6. My soul speaks for my Soulmate 

You came into my life
not to complete me,
but to remind me
that I was already whole—
even in my broken places.

You didn't ask me to be more,
you simply stood close enough
for me to grow into myself.

With you, love is not loud—
it is steady.
It is the way you hold space
for my silence,
and honor the parts of me
I don't always know how to share.

You've heard the language
my soul speaks in stillness—

in the sighs between sentences,
in the quiet tears I never needed to explain.

You've loved me in the pauses,
in the confusion,
in the soft unraveling of who I thought I had to be.

And from that love,
I've rebuilt myself,
not as someone new,
but as someone true.

Because of you,
I no longer fear being seen.
Because of you,
my voice no longer trembles when it's honest.

My soul speaks unsaid—
and in its deepest, most sacred places,
it echoes you.

You are not just in my life.
You are in my becoming.

# 7. Unsaid I am for my birth to mother in me

Newborn you give birth to mother in me.
You came into my life
not just as a gift—
but as a mirror of everything tender,
everything fierce,
everything I never knew lived inside me.

There are no words vast enough
to hold what I feel for you—
only quiet prayers in the dark,
soft whispers to the stars,
and a love that pulses
even when I am silent.

I watch you grow,
and part of me grows with you—
stretching, aching,
learning how to let go
while never truly releasing.

You carry pieces of me
you've never seen—
my strength tucked into your resilience,
my softness curled in your kindness,
my unspoken dreams
woven into your future.

You don't know how often
I've stood behind you,
shielding you with invisible hands,
offering strength
without asking for thanks.

My soul speaks unsaid—
in the sacrifices I never named,
in the joy I found in your joy,
in the way I would break myself
a thousand times
just to see you whole.

You are not just my daughter.
You are my heart turned outward,
my legacy wrapped in light,
my reason to keep becoming.

I am from within—

and because of you,
what lives within me
will live forever.

# 8. I am Introvert I am not erogent

I do not speak to fill the air,
nor smile just to be seen.
My silence is not distance—
it is depth.
A quiet world where I gather meaning
before I give it.

I do not turn away in pride,
I simply turn inward—
where comfort lives,
and chaos softens.

I am not cold.
I am careful.
I listen more than I speak,
and feel more than I show.

Don't mistake my quiet

for judgment.
I am watching,
not weighing.
I am present,
even when I seem far.

I am introvert—
and in my stillness
lives a world
you just haven't entered yet.

# 9. My soul wants to shout and saying I do care 

I walk softly through this world,
not because I have nothing to say,
but because my voice
was born in quiet places.

There is a language
not spoken aloud—
a trembling truth
that lives in glances,
in hesitations,
in the space between words.

I do care.
More than I show,
more than I say.
I care in the way I stay,
in the way I remember,
in the way I carry others in my heart
without needing to be seen.

I may not speak first,
or loudly,
but when I do,
it is always real.

I feel deeply—
sometimes too deeply
for this noisy world.
So I let my silence speak,
let my presence become my voice.

You may not hear me,
but I've been speaking all along—
in kindness unspoken,
in empathy unseen,
in love that doesn't announce itself.

I am not distant.
I am layered.
Not absent—just inward.

My soul speaks unsaid,
and from within,
I give you all I am—
soft, steady,
and quietly full of care.

# 10. I am not short tempered but everyone listen to me like this way only

It murmurs in murmuration,
Woven in the quiet, soft sensation.
Of unseen feelings, deep and true,
Where silence speaks more than words ever do.
It doesn't shout—
It resonates, there's no doubt.
Echoing in places we can't see,
Where words can't touch what's meant to be.
I am not quick to anger—
Though I am met with looks, a little stranger.
As if my calm holds some hidden storm,
When peace is what I feel, what keeps me warm.
They misread my stillness, my quiet way,
Thinking it hides a storm that may.
But I am calm—
A quiet strength, a steady palm.
I do care—

In ways that don't need to share.
In small acts, in moments still,
In silences that show love's will.
My soul speaks
In quiet ways, soft and sleek.
In simple truths, in quiet light,
In moments too deep for words to fight.
I am not gone—
I am here, holding on.
I am not rage—
I am fire, calm and brave.
My soul speaks unsaid,
From within, where truth is led.
It speaks fully—
For those who listen, softly.

# 11. Listen to understand

My soul urging to not advice me ,just understand me.
it utters verses not shaped by tongue,
but etched in the hush
between heartbeats.
I do not wield grand declarations—
I traffic in nuance,
in gestures half-finished,
in glances that long to be deciphered.
I am not tempestuous—
though my truths carry weight,
they are not hurled,
but held.
Yet I am heard
as though I roar.
Perceived as abrupt,
when I am only bare.
*Discern me beyond the surface.*
*Read me not by volume, but by depth.*
*Grant me the grace of comprehension—*
*not just to be heard, but heeded.*

*Perceive me with compassion,*

*not presumption.*

I do care—

in quiet continuums,

in small fidelities,

in ways that often go unseen.

My soul does not beg to be known,

but it does yearn—

to be received,

as it is:

unguarded,

unscripted,

whole.

So if you hear silence,

listen closer.

There is a voice in the stillness,

a storm in the calm,

a plea woven into the quiet:

*Do not merely hear me—*

*understand me.*

# 12. Unintentionally but i hurt you

My soul speaks in quiet ways—
in words I don't always say,
in gestures that go unnoticed.
It speaks from deep inside,
where feelings bubble up but never rush.
It doesn't ask for attention—
it just exists.
I don't get angry easily,
nor do I lose control.
But sometimes,
people read me wrong.
My calmness gets mistaken for coldness,
my confidence seen as judgment.
I'm not trying to start fires—
I'm just being real.
But when I do speak,
it feels like the world pulls back,
as if truth needs to be softened
before it can be heard.

Take your time with me.
Understand my silences as meaning,
not apathy.
And if I've hurt you by accident—
if my quietness cut deeper than I meant,
or my absence felt like rejection—
know that I've carried that hurt too.
I care—
deeply, even if it's not loud.
In the little things,
in words I hold back because I don't know how to say
them.
There's sadness in me,
though it's not always clear—
regret without explanation,
longing without the words to share it.
So when I pull away,
or speak less than I feel—
don't think it's because I don't care.
It's when I'm quietest
that I'm speaking the most—
not in loudness,
but in vulnerability.
Don't just look at me—
try to understand me.
Feel the truth I carry, even if it's not always said.

# 13. Don't regret my presence in your life 

My soul converses in undercurrents,
in the hush behind the heartbeat,
where emotion hums
without the burden of syllables.

I do not flood rooms with sound,
nor parade my truths in the open—
I exist in the in-between,
where nuance lives
and sincerity doesn't shout.

I am not volatile,
but I am vivid.
Not brash,
but unfiltered.

Yet my composure is mistaken for cold,
my clarity mistaken for cruelty.
And still—

I remain.

I extend affection
in imperceptible ways:
in the way I remember your worries,
in the way I stay,
long after it's silent.

If I have ever harmed you
through hesitation,
or let distance settle
where warmth should have lingered—
believe me,
my soul ached where my words failed.
It trembled in the quiet aftermath
of unintended sorrow.

Don't regret my presence in your life.
I brought what was real—
raw, unrehearsed,
sometimes fragmented—
but always rooted in care.

I am not made for performances.
I am made for depth—
for meaning beyond the surface,
for bonds that survive the unspoken.

So, read me slowly.
Feel the intention beneath my quiet.
Not everything I carry wears a name,
but all of it is honest.

My soul speaks unsaid,
and from within,
it offers you a truth
that never needed volume—
only trust.

# 14. Respect is love too

Love Like Respect
Love me like you respect me—
not just in soft whispers,
but in how you listen
when I'm quiet.
Hold me like I'm whole,
not something to fix
or figure out—
but something to value
as I am.
Choose me without control,
speak to me with care,
even when the words are hard.
That's where love lives—
not in flowers,
but in the truth you dare to share.
Touch me with gentleness,
not possession.
Stand beside me,
not over me.

Let your love feel like freedom,
not a cage.
Because real love,
the kind that lasts—
loves like respect,
or it isn't love at all.

# 15. I never said but I want to become a family

Don't love me because you have to,
Or because of what's old or true,
Not because I sit at your table,
Or follow customs when I'm able.
Love me like you respect me,
See the strength inside of me.
Not as an outsider, lost or small,
But as one who loves, and gives her all.
Don't compare me to what's been done,
Or measure me by anyone.
I'm not here to take your place,
But to build, to grow, to share this space.
Speak to me with kindness clear,
With open hearts, no need for fear.
Give me grace, just as you do,
Not more, not less—just equal too.
Because love without respect
Is a bond we cannot protect.
I want more than just to stay,

I want to grow in every way.
I never said, but now I see,
I want to be a family, truly free.
So love me, with respect and cheer,
Together, we'll make a future clear.
And I promise, you will find,
In me, you'll find your family's kind

# 16. Speechless me:You are my beginning

You Are My Beginning
Before you,
I thought I knew love.
But then you arrived—
small, warm,
wrapped in wonder—
and everything changed.
You are my beginning,
my reason to rise,
the softness in my every day.
With one tiny breath,
you filled my world
with meaning.
Your eyes hold galaxies,
your hands, the weight of trust.
And every time you rest on my chest,
the world feels right—
still,
safe,

whole.
I promise to protect you,
to guide you,
to love you in every way I know how—
and even in the ways I'm still learning.
You are not just my baby—
you are my heart,
outside of my body,
forever.

# 17. Let me cry when I want

Let me cry when I want —
not for attention,
not for pity,
but for release.
Sometimes the world feels too loud,
and my heart too full.
Tears are the language
when words fall short.
Don't tell me to be strong.
Strength is not the absence of feeling —
it's the courage to feel it all.
So if you see me breaking,
don't reach to stop the flood.
Just stay.
Breathe with me.
Let the silence hold us both.
Because after the crying,
comes the calm.
And sometimes,

tears are how
I find my way back.

# 18. If I can talk with you
# Runo..

If I could speak and you could hear,
dear Runo, soul so kind and near,
I'd whisper thanks with tear-stained grace,
for every time you held my space.

I never understand your way,
how love from you would never stray.
You knew my heart when words were few,
you stayed—
so silently, so true.

I never do enough, you see,
as you have always done for me.
Your loyalty, your gentle cheer,
your eyes that made my darkness clear.

Runo, if you could speak, you'd say:
"You gave me love in your own way.

I've always known—without a sound,
our souls have met where hearts are found."

# 19. I never ever try to hurt anyone

My intentions are pure for god sake don't misunderstand
me.
I can be harsh at words but can never ever want to hurt
anyone.
I do not speak in thunder—
my voice is made of still water,
my heart, of quiet prayers.

I carry feelings
not in fists,
but in folded hands,
whispering truths
too tender to be loud.

God's promise—
I never try to hurt anyone.
It is not in me
to shatter hearts,
only to mend what's frayed

with the warmth I barely show
but always feel.

If I ever seem distant,
know I am only protecting peace—
yours, mine,
the kind that speaks in silence.

My soul speaks unsaid,
me from within—
not to be loud,
but to be honest,
not to be seen,
but to be felt
in the spaces love never leaves.

# 20. A letter from me Unsaid

To the one who tries to understand me—
There's a version of me
you may never fully hear.
It lives in pauses,
in half-smiles,
in the stillness between my words.
**Unsaid me from within, I cannot express.**
Not because I don't want to—
but because some feelings
aren't shaped for sound.
They exist like stardust:
real, radiant,
but too delicate for language.
I carry warmth in my silences,
apologies in my glances,
and love in the spaces
where my voice gets stuck.
Please know,
I am not distant—just layered.

Not cold—just quiet.
Not indifferent—just cautious
with what is sacred inside me.
If I've ever hurt you by being silent,
it was never my intention.
My soul speaks gently,
often in ways
only the heart can hear.
With all of me—
spoken and unspoken,
visible and hidden—
I am here.
Always.

# 21. I can feel what you think

I speak less,
but I listen beyond sound—
to the tremble in your silence,
to the meaning behind your stillness.

I can feel what you think,
like echoes pressed between glances,
like a wind that moves me
before I know why.

You don't have to explain—
your heart hums in frequencies
only mine seems to catch.
Your joy lights me.
Your hurt unsettles me.

I am the one
who notices your quiet changes,

the shift in your breath,
the weight in your eyes,
the words you almost say.

Unsaid me from within
knows you
not by what you speak—
but by what you hold.

This is not magic.
It is closeness.
It is care turned to instinct,
love turned to knowing.

So even if your voice trembles,
or hides—
just know,
I hear you
in every way
that matters

# 22. When you smile ,my life extending

When you smile, my life extends—
like the sky stretches past where the silence ends.
Time forgets its ticking pace,
and grief dissolves without a trace.

Each curve of light upon your face
revives the parts I can't replace.
Moments I thought were lost for good
bloom again—just like they should.

Your smile is my aura, warm and wide,
a quiet flame I hold inside.
And when it shines, I breathe anew—
as if the world was built for two.

Your smile rewrites my fading lines,
paints new hours on borrowed time.
And in that glance, so soft, so true—
My life extends... because of you.

# 23. I want to live like who I am,

I want to live like who I am,
Not dim my soul, not give a damn
For every gaze that dares to judge
The things I feel, the way I love.

I'm tired of shrinking to fit tight spaces,
Of wearing masks in crowded places.
I crave the freedom to just exist—
No shame, no cage, no need to twist.

Let me be loud, or soft, or strange,
Let me be real, let nothing change
The core of me I've fought to find—
This quiet storm, this vivid mind.

# 24. Unspoken

I want to speak, but silence stays,
A thousand words lost in a haze.
They crowd my chest, they ache, they burn—
Yet every time, the words won't turn.

A trembling breath, a thought begun,
Then swallowed by the setting sun.
My voice retreats, my lips are still—
A prisoner of my own will.

I hold the weight of all I feel,
Like waves beneath a ship's still keel.
Each heartbeat knocks against the cage,
A silent scream, a stifled page.

What if I spoke and shattered peace?
What if I broke and found release?
Would someone hear what hides beneath—
The cracked veneer, the quiet grief?

So here I stay, behind the veil,
My voice a ghost, my thoughts grown pale.
But still, my soul—it longs to shout,
The words I feel, but can't let out.

I fear the weight my truth might bear,
The way it strips me standing there.
No armor left, no practiced lie—
Just naked truth and trembling sky.

What if you turn, or worse, you stay—
But never see me quite that way?
What if my voice, once loosed and free,
Returns unheard—just echoes, me?

So silence holds what heart won't risk,
Each thought preserved like fragile disks.
I carry them, these words unsaid,
Like flowers placed on dreams long dead.

# 25. The Echo of Childhood (Spoken Word)

My soul speaks...
the unsaid me from within—
where childhood whispers still begin.

A softer world.
A smaller hand.
A time I barely understand.

They say time heals.
But it doesn't.
It just hides.
Steals.
Dresses wounds in grown-up lies.

Laughter fades,
but not the place
where love once wore a nameless face.

Repeat that love
I forgot to keep—
the kind that watched me fall asleep.
Before the world
dimmed every light,
before the fear replaced the night.

I carry skies I used to chase,
scraped-up knees,
open space.

My soul still sings those quiet tunes—
cardboard crowns,
paper moons.

But now I walk with practiced grace,
still longing for that vanished place.

My heart?
Still aches in silent skin.
My soul...
it speaks the child
I've locked within.

# 26. I Was Not Wrong

I was not wrong.
But no one stood beside me.
No one said,
"I see you. I believe you."
No one reached out
when I was breaking quietly.

I spoke the truth—
or tried to—
but my voice trembled,
and they mistook it for doubt.

I held pain like a secret,
thinking maybe
someone would hear it
even when I didn't say it out loud.
No one did.

I was not wrong.
But I was alone.

Left to question my own clarity
because no one else
had the courage to agree.

They stayed silent,
not because they didn't know—
but because it was easier
to let me carry it alone.

Still...
I didn't fold.
I didn't turn cruel.
I didn't let their absence
turn me into something I'm not.

So if you're wondering,
if anyone ever asks—
I'll say it clearly now:

I was not wrong.
I was just unheard.
Unseen.
Unsupported.

And that hurts
more than the thing
I was right about.

# 27. A Letter to My Daughter

My sweet girl,

I love you more than anything in this world.
You are a piece of my heart,
a living part of my soul,
and just having you in my life is a gift I never stop being
grateful for.

But there's something I want to say—something honest,
something that's been on my heart.

Sometimes,
I lose my temper with you.
I speak too sharply,
react too quickly,
and I see how it hurts you...
and it breaks me inside.

The truth is, I don't always know why.
It's not about you.

It never has been.

Sometimes it's the pressure,
the tiredness,
the old hurts I've never fully healed.
And sometimes, without meaning to,
I let that weight slip out in ways I regret—especially with
you,
the one I love most.

But please know this:
You are not to blame.
You are not doing anything wrong.
You are full of light, of love, of your own beautiful way
of being.

And I see you.
I see your heart.
I see your strength.
And I'm so, so proud of you.

I'm trying to be better every day—
not just for me, but for you.
You deserve all the patience, kindness, and love I can
give.
And even on the days I fall short,
please never doubt this:

I love you with everything I have,
and I always will.

Forever your mom.

# 28. Behind My Smile

I fight with my inner soul
every single day—
not to say too much,not to let it all slip.

There's a war inside me
of words unsaid, truths buried deep,
feelings locked tight behind practiced peace.

But I wear a smile.
Soft, polite, like everything's alright.
And most people believe it—because they want to.
Because it's easier than asking what's really going on.

They don't see , how heavy silence can be.
They don't hear the arguments I have with myself at 2
a.m.,
convincing my heart to hush.

I wear a smile
even when I ache.

Even when I'm close to breaking.
Because sometimes it feels safer
to seem okay
than to risk falling apart
in front of anyone else.

But just because I'm quiet,
just because I'm calm—
don't think I'm not burning inside.
Don't think I don't wish
someone would look past the smile
and say,
"You don't have to hide here."

# 29. Miss Our Us Time

I miss our us time—
those soft, ordinary hours
where nothing big had to happen
for everything to feel right.

The quiet jokes,
the unspoken rhythm,
the way your hand
always found mine without asking.

I miss the late-night talks,
half-asleep confessions,
the comfort of your voice
sounding like home.

Now life feels louder.
Full of things to do,
places to be,
and somehow less of us

in the middle of it all.

I miss the way we looked at each other
when the world faded away.
The ease,
the laughter,
the calm we carried
just by being close.

I don't know when time started moving so fast—
when silence got heavier
instead of peaceful.
But I feel the space between us.
And I miss you.
Not just your presence—
but the you that was always with me.

I miss our small, sacred things.
The morning coffee.
The glances across the room.
The warmth of knowing
we were each other's safe place.

We're still here.
And that matters.
Even in the distance,
I believe we can find our way back.

Back to softness,
back to laughter,
back to us.

I believe in the love we built—
and I believe
we still belong there.

# 30. Arranged for Love

We didn't fall in love at first sight.
There were no fireworks, no magic spells.
Just two people,
pushed gently together by family,
by hope,
by a little bit of faith.

At first, it was awkward —
half-smiles, careful words,
measuring each other like strangers
who already knew the stakes were high.
But slowly,
your laughter found its way to me.
And I let mine meet it halfway.

We built something —
not out of wild promises,
but out of mornings shared over tea,
arguments over silly things,

forgiveness without needing to say the words.

They called it "arranged,"
but we arranged it, too —
with every small choice to stay,
to listen, to try.

And somehow, somewhere along the way,
what began as a meeting of families
became a meeting of souls.

You are my favorite arrangement.
My favorite accident.
My everyday miracle.

# 31. "For You, With You"

I don't need a bigger reason to live—
I already have you.
You, my little girl,
with your messy hair and endless questions.
You, the man who still looks at me like I'm his whole
world.

I want to live every moment for you.
I want to wake up tired, but still smile because you're
there.
I want to sit on the floor, building castles out of blocks,
even when the world outside forgets how to dream.

I want to be the one who cheers you on,
the one who holds you up,
the one who never leaves.

Some days will be hard—
there will be tears, slammed doors, and heavy silences.
But even then, I will be here.

For you.
With you.

Because you are my every reason.
Because you are the home I didn't even know I was
building.
Because loving you,
both of you,
is the only life I ever wanted.

# 32. Papa. I am Still Your Little Girl

I have a home of my own now, Daddy—
a hand I hold,
a little voice that calls me "Mom."
I kiss scraped knees,
I stay up through long nights,
I carry dreams bigger than I ever thought I could.

But some things haven't changed.

Because when I see you,
I'm still the girl who ran to you with every tear,
the one who believed you could fix the whole world
with just your arms around her.

Even now, with a ring on my finger
and a child in my arms,
there's a part of me that only knows one thing—
I am still yours.

Still the little girl
who needed you to clap the loudest,
who needed your smile to feel brave,
who needed your hugs to breathe easy.

No matter how many birthdays come and go,
no matter how many names I answer to now—
wife, mother, grown-up—
one name will always mean the most:

Daddy's little girl.

And I always will be.

# 33. Life Is Fair — My Thoughts Make It Unfair

Life doesn't owe me anything.
It gives me what it has—
the sun, the rain, the stillness, the chaos.
It's neither kind nor cruel,
it just *is*.
But me? I complicate it.
I worry about what's not yet here,
and miss what's already in front of me.
I make mountains out of small things,
turn peaceful moments into storms.
Life doesn't ask for my approval,
it simply moves on,
while my thoughts create roads
where none need to exist.
Maybe life is fair, after all.
It's my mind that twists it all.

# 34. Why I Can't Forget WHAT I SHOULD

I can't forget,
not for a minute,
'cause my brain's got a habit—
it just won't quit it.
Your laugh's on repeat,
like a song I can't skip,
and every time it plays,
I get pulled back in quick.
I can't forget
the way you smiled,
like you knew something
that made life worthwhile.
My mind's like a playlist,
stuck on track two—
it keeps playing your memory,
even when I don't want it to.
I can't forget,
it's stuck in my head,
like a melody that keeps dancing

while I'm trying to go to bed.
But maybe that's fine,
maybe that's how it's meant to be—
a little piece of you still with me,
humming in harmony.

# 35. Losing is Not the End, Winning is Not the Start

Losing is not the end,
though it feels like a door that's shut,
a fall that leaves you breathless,
and time feels like it's stuck.
But it's just a pause, a breath,
a chance to rise again,
the end is never truly near—
it's just where you begin.
Winning is not the start,
though it feels like the world's at your feet,
a moment that shines so bright,
but it's just another beat.
It's not the start, it's not the end,
it's the journey in between,
where we stumble, where we rise,
and find what lies unseen.

# 36. Just a Moment of Breakdown

It's just a moment,
when everything's too much,
the world feels heavy,
and I've lost my touch.
But this won't last,
it's a pause, not the end,
just a bend in the road
where I have to mend.
I can see the light,
the days full of cheer,
when laughter's the rhythm,
and joy's all I'll hear.
So I'll breathe through this,
and let it pass by,
because after the storm,
the sun will still rise.
It's just a moment,
and soon I'll be strong,
with happy hours ahead,

and life moving on.
But if nobody cares,
why should I still fight?
Why keep pushing forward
when they won't see the light?
Why live for their sake,
if they don't see the truth,
if I'm just another face,
lost in their pursuit?
Yet I know in my heart,
I'm worth more than this,
there's life still to live,
and joy still to kiss.
I'll stand through the storm,
and fight for my name,
because no one else can
ignite my flame.
I know I'll smile again,
feel warmth in my soul,
like the first rays of morning,
taking back control.
So I'll let the tears fall,
they're only part of the way,
the rain makes the flowers
that bloom after the gray.
This moment will fade,
just like the night does to dawn,

and I'll stand taller, stronger,
knowing I've moved on.
It's just a moment of breakdown,
but my heart's built to rise,
and with each step I take,
I'll find my happy skies.
And in the end, I'll be free—
happy, carefree, just being me.
No longer trapped by doubt or fear,
I'll laugh and live without a tear.

# 37. Unappreciated, Yet Still Standing (Neurophysiotherapist & Professor)

I walk into the clinic,
tired but hopeful,
knowing the weight each body carries,
the stories that words don't speak.
I guide their hands,
their legs, their hearts—
trying to remind them that healing
is a quiet journey,
one step, one breath, one trust at a time.
But sometimes, I wonder—
who sees the hours,
the moments I stay late,
when everyone else has gone home,
still listening, still caring,
even when no one asks.

As a professor, I stand before them,
sharing everything I know,
hoping they feel what I feel—
this deep, quiet love for the body,
for the mind, for every moment of progress.
But there's no thank-you,
no recognition in the rush,
just more work to do,
more names to grade,
more students who may forget
the quiet sacrifices I've made.
And when the paycheck comes,
it doesn't match the price I've paid—
the late nights, the endless care,
the moments I've given,
the love I've shared.
I'm expected to heal,
to teach, to guide,
but the salary falls short,
the value lost in the tide.
No reflection of the work I do,
the lives I touch, the hours I give—
and yet, I continue,
because I choose to live.
In every touch,
in every word I say,
I am giving a part of myself—

a part of my heart,
my soul, my quiet strength,
that they may never see.
I may not wear a badge of honor,
or have the loud applause,
but I feel the difference I make—
in every smile, in every step,
in the way their pain begins to fade.
So I stand,
even when the world is silent,
even when my name is never spoken with gratitude,
even when my work is undervalued,
because I know the truth within me—
I heal, I teach, I give with love.
Unappreciated, yes—
but still, I rise,
with my heart wide open,
knowing that somewhere, somehow,
the impact I've made will live on,
long after the applause fades away.

# 38. Why I Show That I Got Hurt

Why do I show it—
the pain I try to hide?
When deep inside,
I wish I could just slide.
I wear my hurt like a cloak,
for all to see,
hoping someone might notice,
hoping someone will care for me.
I speak the truth,
though it's hard to say,
'Cause keeping it in
just makes me fade away.
I don't want to look weak,
but pretending gets tough—
Sometimes showing my hurt
is the way I feel enough.
Why do I let you see my tears?
When I'd rather bury them deep,
pretend I'm fine,

and hide the pain I keep.
But maybe I show it
'cause I'm tired of the fight,
of carrying this burden
and hiding from the light.
I show that I got hurt—
it's how I start to heal,
in the act of sharing
is where I can feel real.
Maybe I need someone,
to see me just as I am,
to tell me it's okay to break,
and to help me stand.
So, I show that I got hurt,
not for pity, not for pride,
but just to feel connected,
and no longer try to hide.
I don't need to be fixed,
I just need to be seen,
and in that moment of truth,
I'll stop feeling so unseen.

# 39. Your Words Are Temporary, But They Hurt More

Your words are fleeting,
but their weight lingers long—
a sting that stays even when
you've moved on.
A moment's thought,
a careless phrase—
and suddenly, I'm lost,
in an ocean of your gaze.
You don't see the crack
in the heart you just tore,
because you were speaking in haste,
but I'm left aching at the core.
You'll forget what you said,
just another fleeting sound,
but I'm left holding the pieces,
drowning in what I found.
It's funny how something so light,

can cut so deep,
how something you said without thinking,
can make me lose sleep.
Your words are temporary,
but the hurt stays still,
like a shadow that follows me
against my will.
I wish I could let them go,
like you so easily do,
but the echo of your words
keeps ringing through.
I don't need apologies,
or words to take it back,
I just need to understand
why you left me with the lack.
Your words may fade,
but the scars remain,
and I'll carry them with me,
in joy, in loss, in pain.

# 40. I Am a Mom, But I Need My Mom Too

I am a mom,
with hands that hold and guide,
I give my all,
with love that never hides.
I comfort the cries,
I kiss away the fears,
I'm the one they turn to,
to calm all their tears.
But there are days—
when I'm feeling small,
when the weight of it all
feels too heavy to call.
I am the strong one,
the rock they cling to,
but inside I wonder,
who will hold me too?
I give and I give,
but sometimes I ache,
for the touch of a hand

that helps me unbreak.
I'm the one who comforts,
but who comforts me?
When I need a shoulder,
when I need to just be.
I need my mom too,
to see the silent tears,
to remind me it's okay
to face my own fears.
I want to rest,
to be held for a while,
to hear her soft words,
and see her gentle smile.
But I'm a mom now,
I'm the one they rely on,
yet deep in my heart,
I still wish I could be her son.
I am strong,
but I am human too,
I need her like I always did—
just to see me through.

# 41. God, Give Me My Elder Sister, My Forever Friend

God, give me my elder sister,
the one who lights my way,
the one who guides with gentle hands
through every night and day.
Not just a sister by blood,
but the friend who holds my soul,
the one who's walked before me,
helping me become whole.
Her wisdom is my compass,
her love my steady ground,
she's the voice of calm when chaos comes,
the peace when I'm unbound.
She's the one I run to,
when the world feels far too much,
the one who knows my heart's quiet cries,
with just a gentle touch.
God, give me the sister I need,
the one who teaches me to stand,
who shows me strength in every step

with a guiding, loving hand.
Her laughter is a balm to me,
her smile a steady flame,
I pray her love will never fade,
and that she'll always remain.
God, give me my elder sister,
my forever friend,
the one whose heart and wisdom
help me heal and transcend.
Because in her, I find my mirror,
and through her, I find my way,
an elder sister, always and forever,
my friend, come what may.

# 42. I Don't Have Friends, But I Am Happy

I don't have friends,
but I'm learning to smile,
finding joy in my own company,
walking my own mile.
The silence doesn't scare me,
it's where I find my peace,
in the quiet of my own heart,
where all my worries cease.
I watch the world around me,
and though I may be alone,
I realize happiness doesn't need
someone to call my own.
I don't have friends,
but I am happy still,
because I've found a love inside me,
that no one can distill.
I've learned to laugh at my own jokes,
and dance when no one's near,
I've found a rhythm in my soul

that brings me joy and cheer.
I don't have friends,
but I don't feel the lack,
for I am whole within myself,
and that's a love that won't turn back.
Perhaps someday someone will come,
but until then, I'm free,
to walk this journey with a smile,
loving who I've come to be.

# 43. And I Have High Blood Pressure(:

I have high blood pressure,
It's a thing, it's real,
My heart's a race car,
And I'm behind the wheel!
The doc says, "Take it easy,"
But stress is everywhere,
I try to find peace,
But it's just not there!
Tea's my best friend,
Stress is my foe,
But when I try to relax,
My blood pressure says "Hello!"
I eat my leafy greens,
I pop my pills with grace,
But every time I check the news,
I'm in a different race!
My heart's doing gymnastics,
My head's in a spin,
I just need a nap,

Or maybe some gin?
I walk, I stretch,
I try to be zen,
But then I stub my toe,
And it starts all over again!
I'll laugh it off, though,
One step at a time,
With my blood pressure rising,
But hey, I'll still rhyme.
So here's to my blood pressure,
I'll live with the stress,
I'm high on life—
But I guess not my BP, yes?

# 44. Expectations Always Hurt

I walked in thinking, "This is it, I'm on top!"
Then the universe laughed—like, "Nah, just stop."
I expected a text—got a typo instead,
I thought I'd shine—turns out I just bled.
I planned to be on time—oh, how I tried,
But my shoes had other plans—can't blame the ride.
I thought I'd coast through—smooth as can be,
But my coffee fought back—guess it wasn't meant to be.
I expected calm—found chaos instead,
I thought I'd win—nah, I tripped on my head.
I thought I'd have it all figured out by now,
But life's just a circus, and I'm here for the show—
somehow.
I expected peace—but found a storm to chase,
I planned for a sprint—ended up with a race.
I thought I'd find the perfect way to be,
But all I've got is messy, and honestly, it's free.
So yeah, my plans are like bad Wi-Fi—never quite clear,
But at least I'm here, and I'll keep shifting the gear.

Expectations hurt—but here's the thing,
They set us up to fly when we learn how to swing.
So when life throws a curveball, just laugh and say,
"Guess I'll try again—I'm good, anyway."
Because falling down? It's just part of the play,
And after every misstep, you'll find your way.
Expectations hurt—but they're just part of the ride,
So buckle up, laugh loud, and enjoy the tide.

# 45. I Accept Myself

I accept that I'm not perfect,
and I'm okay with being worth it.
I don't have to get it all,
because I rise when I fall.
I accept that I make mistakes,
but I learn from what it takes.
Each misstep doesn't define me,
it refines me—can't you see?
I accept that some days are rough,
but I'm tougher than enough.
When the road gets hard to climb,
I'll still rise—every time.
I accept that I'm not always calm,
but I'll find peace and stay strong.
Through the chaos, I'll breathe deep,
and let my inner courage keep.
I accept that I'm still in bloom,
growing, changing, finding room.
I don't need to be flawless to shine,
I just need to keep on my line.

So here I stand, flaws and all,
knowing I'll rise, and never fall.
I accept myself, and I'm proud,
I'm strong, and I'll say it out loud.

# 46. I Should Be the Only One Who Makes or Breaks Me

I spent too long believing you held the key,
like you could unlock the parts I couldn't see.
I tried to fit in, make myself easy to be,
but I'm not something you can mold or decree.
I'm not paper—don't fold me so easily,
I'll bend, but I don't break, I promise you'll see.
I'm more than the quiet, the safe, the plea—
I'm the storm that rises, the wild, the free.
You can't box me in, can't claim what's mine to be,
I'll fill up the space where I once let you be.
If I crumble, I'll find a way back, just wait and see,
for I'm the only one who can make or break me.
I've learned the hard way—my power's not for sale,
my strength isn't something that's here to fail.
I'll rise from the ashes, I'll fly without a trail,
I'm the one who writes my story, no need to tell.
I'll make my own road, whether smooth or frail,

and if I stumble, I'll laugh, I won't wail.
I'll be the fire, the force, the wind in the sail—
because I'm the only one who can make or break this
tale

# 47. Don't Want to Wake Up the Robot in Me

I don't want to wake up the robot in me,
'Cause once it's up, I'm as stiff as can be.
I'll start calculating my coffee-to-sleep ratio,
And forget how to smile—it's a full-on show.
I don't want to reboot and check my settings,
Or give my emotions a system of settings.
One wrong move, and I'm in auto-mode,
Where all I do is work, then go in "sleep" mode.
If I push "on" before 9 a.m.,
I'll be stuck on "processing" again and again.
I don't need algorithms to track my mood,
I need a nap and some good food.
So please, don't hit "activate" too soon—
Or I'll start calculating how to avoid the moon.
I don't need a glitch in my daily routine,
I just need a break from my human machine.
So let's keep the wires to a minimum today—
Let the robot stay asleep and enjoy the play.

The world can wait while I'm on "standby" mode,
I'll recharge, and I'll be ready to load!

# 48. I Never Get What I Want On Time

I never get what I want on time,
But that's okay, I'll still climb.
Plans may shift, and dreams may stall,
But I'll keep going—standing tall.
I asked for five minutes of rest,
But I'll take an hour and do my best.
I may be behind, but I'm not out of place,
I'll keep moving forward at my own pace.
I set my goals, I make my list,
And sometimes the timing doesn't exist.
But every step is still progress made,
I'm learning patience, every delay.
I wait for answers, I wait for signs,
But I know the best things take their time.
I'll keep on pushing, one step more,
Because success is built on what we endure.
The package might come late, that's fine,
I'm building something—just give it time.
My dreams are coming, just wait and see,

Even if they don't arrive immediately.
I may not get there in a flash,
But I'll get there, I'll make a splash.
The clock can tick, but I'll take the time,
To reach my goals—and make them mine.
So here's to the delays, the waiting game,
I'll keep my focus, and fan the flame.
Timing may not always be on my side,
But I'll keep striving—my dreams won't hide.

# 49. I Am Hard to Define, But Easy to Understand

I'm hard to define, a spark in the dark,
A blend of mystery, but I've left my mark.
I can't be boxed in, I break the mold,
But I'm simple to see—if you're brave and bold.
I'm unpredictable, and that's my strength,
I'll keep you on your toes, but I'll go the length.
Sometimes quiet, sometimes loud,
But I rise above, I stand proud.
I don't fit the standards, I'm a force of my own,
But I'm grounded, and my roots have grown.
I may not follow the rules, I might make my own,
But you'll see my heart, it's carved in stone.
I might leave you curious, make you pause,
But my essence is clear—no hidden laws.
I'm a puzzle, but the pieces fall into place,
Once you understand, you'll embrace my pace.
I'm not here to conform, I won't play that game,
But my spirit is strong, and it will never wane.
You might not know what I'll do next,

But you'll know I'm unstoppable—complex yet direct.
So call me unique, call me one of a kind,
I'm my own force—no need to rewind.
You may not always understand right away,
But keep watching, I'll light the way.

# 50. Life is Short, But Live for Infinity

Life is short, but don't be afraid,
In every moment, the earth is swayed.
We plant our deeds like seeds in the ground,
In nature's embrace, we're truly found.
What we do may hide from others' eyes,
But our actions speak truth, no disguise.
We can't outrun the things we've done,
For in our hearts, we're the only one.
Confess your wrongs, correct your course,
Before regret takes its endless force.
For time moves on, no pause, no brake,
And once it's gone, there's no mistake.
The clock ticks on, but we don't race,
We walk through life with steady grace.
Our actions ripple through the sky,
Like rivers flowing, reaching high.
Life's a spark, but we're the flame,
A fleeting moment, but we leave no shame.
In every tree, in every breeze,

Our deeds live on with nature's ease.
So live like the sun that paints the day,
With deeds of love, we find our way.
Life is short, but love is long,
In every leaf, we sing our song.
Live with purpose, just like the sea,
Flowing endlessly, wild and free.
Though time may fade, our roots remain,
We live for infinity, in truth we reign.

# 51. I Am Listening, Just Say

I am listening, just say,
Your voice can light the way.
Don't hold back, don't hesitate,
Speak your truth—it's never too late.
Every word has power within,
A spark of strength, a place to begin.
Speak with courage, speak with pride,
I'm here, ready to stand by your side.
I am listening, just believe,
The dreams you have, you can achieve.
Let your thoughts rise, let them soar,
With each word, you'll find more.
No need for silence, no need to fear,
Your voice matters, it's crystal clear.
I am listening, speak your mind,
Together, we'll leave doubt behind.

www.ingramcontent.com/pod-product-compliance
Lightning Source LLC
LaVergne TN
LVHW050912200726
843508LV00011B/2184